IN PLAIN SIGHT
HOW THE EPISTEMOLOGY OF IGNORANCE NORMALIZES GENDER-BASED VIOLENCE

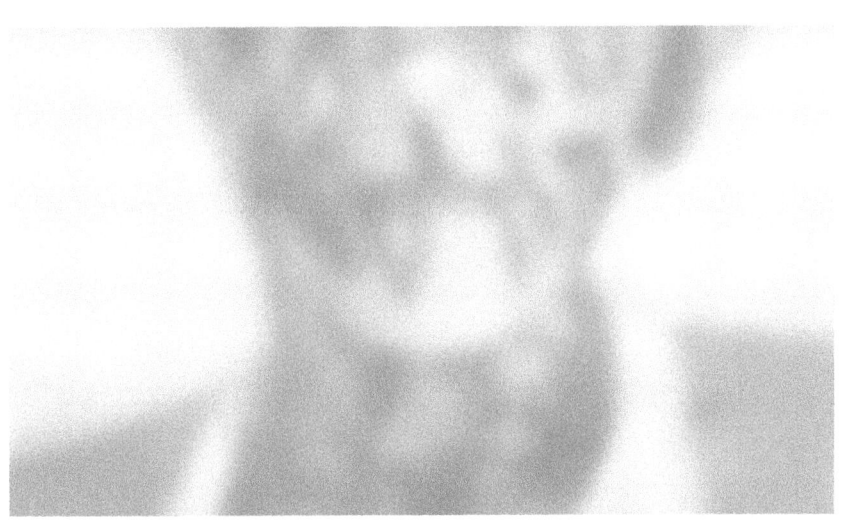

Mary Simmerling, Ph.D.

Copyright ©2025 ….. MARY SIMMERLING

ALL RIGHTS RESERVED: No part of this publication may be reproduced, stored in a retrieval system or transmitted in any form or by any means without prior written permission from the publisher and the author.

Editor: MARY SIMMERLING, Ph.D.

Cover Image: © Mary Simmerling, Self-portrait, Ink on skin.

Interior Art: © Mary Simmerling, Self-portrait, Charcoal on paper + Self-portrait, Ink on skin. © Mary Simmerling, Winter Cattails, Photo.

Cover Design & Interior Layout: Sarah Pierson

Editing & Manuscript Development: Meadow Jones, Ph.D.

Published by:
    WRITE WHERE WE BELONG PRESS
    OTTAWA ON Canada
    writewherewebelong.ca

ISBN 978-1-0688285-6-0 pbk
ISBN 978-1-0688285-7-7 ebook

Author's Note

The poems in this book emerge from a deeply personal and creative process, in which lived experiences and memories have been drawn upon and transformed through the art of poetry. They are expressed with the imaginative license that is central to the craft, including through the use of metaphor. While many elements are inspired by real events and relationships, they have been reimagined and articulated in a manner that transcends a mere factual recounting. The poems should be interpreted figuratively rather than literally. The essays and poems in this book are intended as cultural and literary criticism, offering commentary on societal issues through artistic expression.

TABLE OF CONTENTS

Introduction	15
A Paucity of Language	20
Analytic Dialectic	23
Language Games	25
They Are Rewriting Our Stories	27
At the Gas Station	28
Chewing Barbed Wire	31
At Risk	33
No One Talks Much Anymore	36
IN ORDER—	38
The Brutalists	39
Mercy	41
"Prostitutes": A Pernicious Misnomer	47
Traffic	50
I Wonder What it is I Am Supposed to Do	53
In the Company of Women	55
Hunting Grounds	57
These Things	59
Give Us Back Our Names	63
Requiem for Girls	70
Remains	72
Rats	74
Nothing to See Here	79
Monster	85
The Haunting Hours	86
In Plain Sight	89
Sparrows on a Clothesline	92
Thought Experiment	94
Resources	101
References and Further Reading	105

With deep respect and gratitude for the life and transformational contributions of Charles W. Mills, Ph.D.—mentor, scholar, friend.

For the invisible and erased, and those who refuse to look away.

IN PLAIN SIGHT:
HOW THE EPISTEMOLOGY OF IGNORANCE NORMALIZES GENDER-BASED VIOLENCE

A rat in a maze is free to go anywhere, as long as it stays inside the maze.

Ignoring isn't the same as ignorance, you have to work at it.

— Margaret Atwood, *The Handmaid's Tale*

Charles W. Mills, Ph.D.
January 3, 1951 - September 20, 2021

Author's Note: In Memory of Charles W. Mills, Ph.D.

When I visited my alma mater, the University of Illinois at Chicago, last fall, I hadn't been prepared to learn that my beloved mentor Charles Mills had died. Not that we had stayed in contact very often over the 20 years since I completed my Ph.D., but I kept track of his work and saw that at some point he'd left Chicago and taken a distinguished faculty role in NYC. During the pandemic I had reached out to him to see how he was doing and what he was working on. I never heard back from him. What I didn't know was that he was already gone by then. At the time, I was studying his work in a psychology graduate class with a brilliant Black hip hop scholar - Solomon Commissiong - who was teaching courses on social justice. He was blown away when I said, "I love Charles Mills - he was on my dissertation committee."

I still remember when Charles offered to be on my dissertation committee. He said my name the way he always did with his gorgeous Jamaican accent, asking, "Mary, why haven't you asked me to be on your committee?" It had never occurred to me that he cared about and respected my work enough to take me on as one of his own. But he had and he did. His 1997 book *The Racial Contract* was an adaptation and extension of Carole

Pateman's 1988 book *The Sexual Contract*. In *The Racial Contract*, Charles wrote about how racism was built into the patriarchy, and detailed the ways in which patriarchal systems subjugate nonwhites and women as "lesser" and "other." He coined the phrase "the epistemology of ignorance" to describe how privileged groups remain willfully ignorant of the mechanisms that sustain their dominance, and the ways in which this allows them to overlook and misrepresent nonwhites and women's experiences of agency.

Back in Chicago last year, I sat in my former advisor David Hilbert's office, weeping together over the loss of Charles. David had been another profound influence on my intellectual life, and together we remembered the impact Charles had on both of us and shared stories about his humility and generosity, as well as his unmatched intellectual and scholarly expertise. I still remember the night I dropped a printout of my final dissertation chapter at his apartment in Evanston. As I drove back into the city, the sky lit up with fireworks. While I knew they weren't for me, it felt like a celebration nonetheless, and like Charles was cheering me on.

In remembering Charles and his groundbreaking work and legacy, a title came to mind for a collection of essays and poems I had been writing about gender-based violence and society's willful turning away from the reality of it—a way to honor his work and continue it through my own In Plain Sight: How the Epistemology of Ignorance Normalizes Gender-Based Violence. This is the book you are now reading. In it, I have endeavored to apply Charles's framework of an epistemology of ignorance to gender-based violence in my own words and in my own way, showing how patriarchal structures silence, distort, and erase women's experiences of harm. This book continues Charles's essential work by exposing how patriarchal structures sustain dominance through willful ignorance—silencing, distorting, and erasing women's experiences of harm and agency.

Mary Simmerling
Ottawa, Ontario
25 February 2025

IN PLAIN SIGHT:
HOW THE EPISTEMOLOGY OF IGNORANCE NORMALIZES GENDER-BASED VIOLENCE

Introduction

We must confront the reality that gender-based violence is a public health crisis—one we can no longer ignore. Globally, one in three women will experience gender-based violence in their lifetime. Every day, 137 women are killed by family members, and one billion children suffer abuse each year. In 2020 alone, the UN reported that 47,000 women and girls were murdered by intimate partners or other family members—on average, one every 11 minutes. Every day. These figures do not include perpetrators who are acquaintances or strangers. While these numbers have remained largely unchanged for the past decade, a 2024 report from the United Nations Office on Drugs and Crime identified a staggering 25% increase in this number based in large part on an increase in the number of children being trafficked.

Research from the Canadian Femicide Observatory for Justice and Accountability found that in Canada, a woman or girl is murdered every 2.5 days. Indigenous women are 12 times more likely to be killed or to be reported missing, yet these cases remain disproportionately unresolved. These numbers are staggering—and unacceptable. They are more than statistics. They are lives. And they are being taken—primarily by men.

They have names, like Laken Riley. The fact that Laken Riley's killer was found guilty in a court of law by a male judge will not right this terrible loss. Her mother will forever know that she missed a phone call that might have delayed her daughter leaving for her run. That might have prevented her from being captured and murdered by Jose Ibera. But as the prosecutor in the case said (Silva, 2024), Ibera was out hunting for a woman that morning. He was laying in wait in the woods. And when he saw Laken, he captured and killed her. If it hadn't been Laken, it would have been someone else. A different woman or girl with a different name and a different mother now left forever grieving at an altar of despair.

This violence is preventable. These deaths are preventable. I wonder what it will take for us to wake up to the reality of the pervasive and widespread epidemic of violence against women and children. Just as we mobilized resources and attention to address other preventable public health crises - like COVID-19, tobacco, and polio - we must confront violence against women and children with the same urgency. The time is now.

MARY SIMMERLING

MARY SIMMERLING

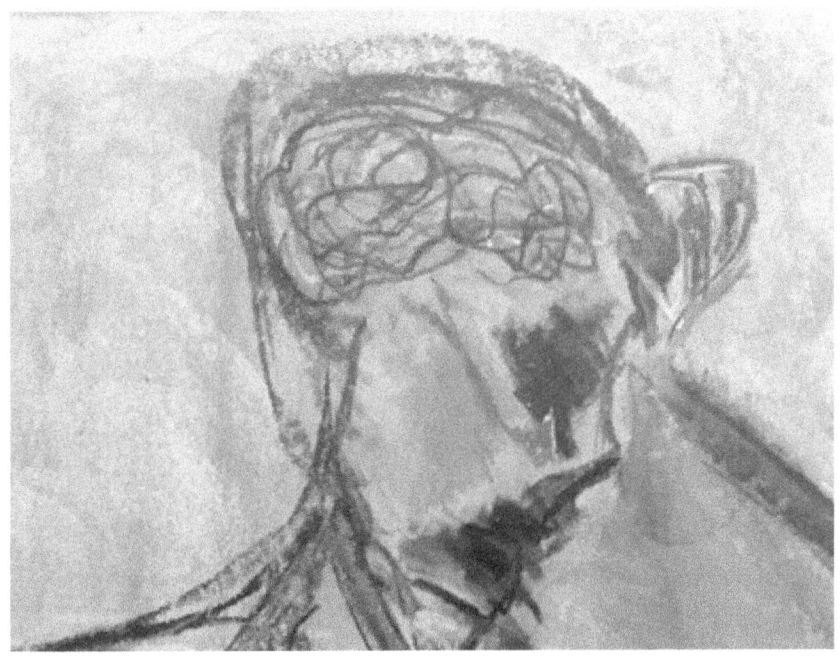

A Paucity of Language

Like many survivors of sexual violence, for years I lacked the very language in which to talk about what had happened to me. Someone once asked me why I didn't scream– and I wanted to say that I hadn't had a voice then. And I wondered how it was that they could have not known that. The screams came for me later— in the middle of the night, waking up alone and afraid. Afraid of the silence. Afraid of the dark. Afraid of the night. Alone in the silence. Like so many other survivors of sexual violence, I had been left alone in silence for so long that at some point I realized that it had engulfed me.

As I wrote in *We've Been Put Through Fire & Come Out Divine,* survivors' voices have been silenced for so long, we have been told that our truths aren't true, and that even if they were, no one cares anyway. And in response, we have hidden, made ourselves small, and become silent and invisible. Left alone without conversations through which we can interrogate what has happened to us, a lexicon is foisted onto us that is centered around blame and shame. It is the lexicon of the perpetrator, not the victim. This lexicon of lies is not only forced onto survivors, it is forced into us in yet another violation, because of the many ways in which it is systematically reinforced at every turn, to the point that survivors come to internalize these false narratives. We are fed language and given tools to parse all the seemingly endless ways in which we are responsible for what has happened to us. We are asked accusatory questions such as— *What were you wearing? Aren't you dating? How much had you been drinking?* These thinly veiled accusations also beg the question of whether a victim could ever be culpable by implicitly assuming that rape could ever be justified or deserved—for example, whether rape might be an appropriate punishment for intoxication, which it unequivocally is not.

This language seeks to skew and distort the discourse about what has happened to us, and in so doing to further disempower us. It seeks to place the burden on us as survivors by attempting to shift the blame and shame for what has happened to us onto us. But it doesn't have to continue to be the language we use to talk about these events, who is actually to blame for them, and the lasting impact they have on the lives of survivors. Instead, we need a new language—a new rubric that will help us to articulate and understand the wide range of events that constitute sexual violence. We need to stop parsing the facts that surround sexual violence and instead place the blame directly onto the predators themselves. Continued use of terms such as "date rape" and "incest" seek to draw our attention away from the facts of these acts of sexual violence and instead redirect our focus onto the relationship between the perpetrator and the victim, as if the victim is somehow complicit because of the relationship to the perpetrator. For example, a father and a daughter, a sister and brother, romantic partners, or other intimate relationships.

Psychotherapist and author Edy Nathan's (2024) innovative terminology of "predatory events" that grew out of her work identifying and describing the "sexual grief effect" provides just such an expansive rubric through which we can begin to lift the silence and shame and give survivors back their stories. This language also creates space in which survivors of predatory events can engage in meaningful conversations about the truth of what has happened to them and the devastating impact it has had on their lives, leaving what Nathan has accurately described as a "traumatic imprint." Leveraging this innovative new language allows us to expand the currently limited conceptions of sexual violence to include events that do not necessarily involve physical contact, such as stalking, harassment, and artificially manufactured sexually explicit materials that cause similar harms and create violent repercussions. As Susanne Kappler (1986) observed:

> "Representations are not just a matter of mirrors, reflections, keyholes. Somebody is making them, and somebody is looking at them..."

The blast radius of these events is woefully underestimated and remains poorly understood. This is due in large part to the lack of a precise language with which we can talk about these predatory events, and the impact they have on victims, survivors, and the communities in which they exist. Nathan describes some of these effects, including the grief, self-loathing, self-blame, and disgust that emerge as a natural response to predatory events, thus illuminating how the shame presents itself for survivors. We need to do better. We need to look harder. We need to talk about what it is that we see— to accurately describe it. And if the words do not yet exist, we need to create them.

Analytic Dialectic

Sometimes

words take away

rather than give

meaning

degrade

rather than elaborate

insidiously

almost imperceptibly

carving away

at those around them

seducing us

by masquerading as if

they are adding

something important

some moral force

expression of repugnance

defying us

even as

we speak them aloud

record them

in print

anesthetizing us

to the intrinsic brutalities

of violence and aggression

leaving us

in the end

with less

rather than more

less truth

less reality

less humanity.

See for yourself:

she was forcibly raped

and brutally beaten.

Language Games

At lunch we split into groups
of two, three, or more

a break from the day's routine
which was otherwise quiet and stationary.

As I walked by their table
I heard him say

(bitterly
and in too loud a voice)

She's so opinionated
and she thinks she can
get away with it
just because she's smart.

Knees shaking a bit now
I sat back down
at my table
and invented a game.

Here's how to play:
try to put the same sentence
back in someone's mouth
but with the pronouns
switched.

Sometimes it can transform

an accusation

into so much nonsense

by replacing just a single word.

(It's like magic really!)

Watch this:

he's so opinionated

and he thinks he can get away with it

just because he's smart.

They Are Rewriting Our Stories

They are rewriting
our stories

culled from
their websites

altering our genders
without permission.

We must stand
against them—

we must stand
together
against them.

Every organization
that once protected

unrecognizable
distorted
and barren.

They are rewriting
our stories

without
our permission.

At the Gas Station

I hadn't even made it

through the door

when suddenly

she was there—

having rushed to my side

reaching out

as if she needed me

desperately

as if she'd been waiting

for me

to arrive.

Her eyes

searched mine

I could feel the heat

of her breath

as she said—

I cannot believe it

I cannot believe

that they picked him

how did they pick him?

It must be a mistake—
how is this possible
how is this even possible?

I could feel her rage

meet mine

as if we were

inside

the same body

standing together

in the shop

at the gas station—

for a moment

time

evaporated

everything else

ceased

to exist.

She returned

to her place

behind the counter.

Large men
came and went

buying beef jerky
cigarettes and beer
diesel for their trucks

Nonplussed—

they did not
share our rage.

They did not
feel
the terror
we felt.

They did not
seem to understand

that they are coming
for them
too—

they are coming for them too.

Chewing Barbed Wire

It is

an algorithm
of erasure

a systematic
removal

(No man does it all
on his own)

an unmooring
from the self.

I wonder
what it is they are doing—

with their
single fists
clenched and raised

arms jutting out
at familiar angles

feet shuffling to
stolen songs

(They have everything for the men to enjoy
come and hang out with all the boys).

In the dark
I whisper
to myself

(every thought
I have—)

sedition.

They say they will
protect us

whether we like it
or not

(Young men
there's no need to be down—
you can do whatever it is you feel.)

At Risk*

They privilege:

status

exclusion

hate speech

racism

segregation

injustice

polarization

systemic inequality

pollution

health disparity.

Biases:

historically

undervalued

underserved—

women

minorities

vulnerable populations
trauma victims

social justice
racial justice.

Most risk:

underprivileged
females

tribal
Black

minorities
immigrants

climate science
clean energy.

All-inclusive barriers:

institutional discrimination
oppressive stereotypes

cultural heritage
confirmation bias.

MARY SIMMERLING

Excluded:

equal opportunity
mental health

female victims'
sexual preferences

gender identity
they/them

belonging
sense of belonging.

*This poem is composed entirely of words included on the list of disappearing terms identified in the March 7, 2025 The New York Times article "These Words Are Disappearing in the New Trump Administration" by K. Yourish, A. Daniel, S. Datar, I. White, and L. Gamio.

No One Talks Much Anymore

Including me.

These days
to speak
is to engage
in sedition—

it is the only reason
to speak

the truth

elusive
and urgent

an algorithm
of erasure.

What do you have to say about them taking those words off their website, he demanded—

We must not allow them to capitulate — we must now organize against them — who is with me, she implored—

Traps
laid
and baited

turning against
each other

turning away
from them

distracted
exhausted.

Back in the cave
with its shadows--

the truth
elusive
and distorted

by shame
and silence.

No one talks much
anymore.

IN ORDER—

PROHIBIDO EL PASO

禁止入内

BAWAL PUMASOK

CẤM VÀO

ممنوع الدخول

DÉFENSE D'ENTRER

출입 금지

ВХОД ВОСПРЕЩЁН

ANTRE ENTÈDI

EINTRITT VERBOTEN

प्रवेश निषेध

PROIBIDA A ENTRADA

立入禁止

VIETATO L'INGRESSO

ZAKAZ WSTĘPU

داخلہ منع ہے

ورود ممنوع

પ્રવેશ પ્રતિબંધિત

ప్రవేశం నిషిద్ధం

প্রবেশ নিষেধ

(NO ENTRY)

(NO RETURN)

The Brutalists

A carefully

crafted

execution

architected

for years

dark scaffolding

ropes knotted

and looped.

Still—

they walk

red carpets

cameras

flashing

preternaturally white

smiles

pressed suits

sculpted shoulders

jewels lighting

winter suntans

never stopping

to wonder

what will happen

when

the help

(long hidden)

are

scooped up

caged

and

evicted.

Mercy

If it is true

that holiness does not

dissolve—

I want to know

what happens

when I cannot

see it.

Surely

it is fearless

but where does it go—

those times

when it seems to have

disappeared?

I watch as

hate spreads

like wildfires

scorching

the land of the free.

I do not

recognize

this place

with its fear

and anger.

Wherefore

the hearts

yearning

to breathe

free?

What of the land

that loved

mercy

more than

life?

Return again

open us—

let us

be spacious

and brave

as we search out

a balm

to heal

our wounded souls.

Under beautifully

indivisible skies

that cannot

be taken

away.

IN PLAIN SIGHT:
HOW THE EPISTEMOLOGY OF IGNORANCE NORMALIZES GENDER-BASED VIOLENCE

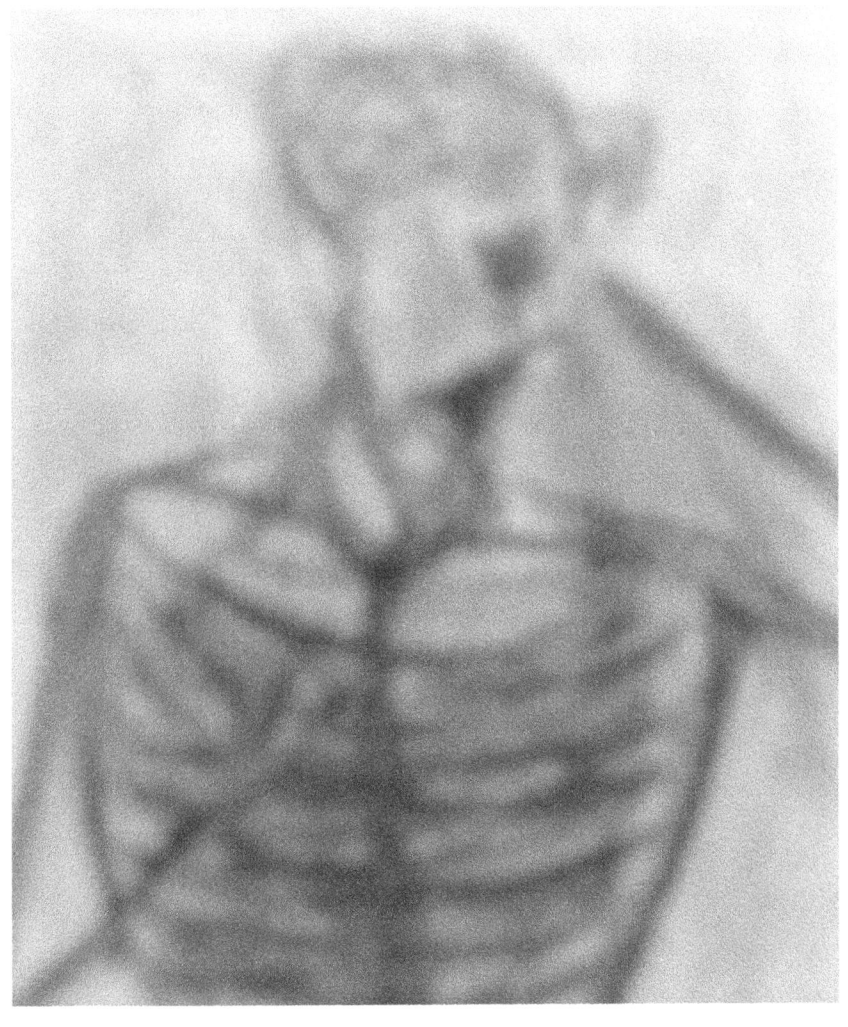

IN PLAIN SIGHT:
HOW THE EPISTEMOLOGY OF IGNORANCE NORMALIZES GENDER-BASED VIOLENCE

"Prostitutes": A Pernicious Misnomer

Looking at a photo of an odometer the other day reminded me that I'm still thinking about that "Parking Meter" poem, and the feedback I got about the piece I wrote in response to it. In the original piece, the poet seems to compare prostitution to the act of feeding a parking meter, implying paying for parking is like paying for time with a prostitute (Tuck, 2024). I was told that my response to piece - a poem called "Traffic" - was "too hot" and needed to cool down a bit. So I let it sit. And I thought about ways to cool it down. But it stayed hot. And so I started researching the elusive and woefully incomplete statistics currently available about the percentage of women and girls who are "prostitutes."

Here is some of what I learned: Of the 4.8 million people who are sex trafficked each year, 94-99% of them are women and girls (International Labour Organization, 2017; United Nations Office on Drugs and Crime, 2020). And overall, a substantial percentage of these women and girls "in prostitution" or what is now called "sex work" - I can barely even stand to write that - are victims of human trafficking. So that means between 4.5 and 4.75 million women and girls are trafficked for the purpose of sexual assault each year (International Labour Organization, 2017; United Nations Office on Drugs and Crime, 2020). They are not "prostitutes" or "sex workers" by choice, but instead because they have been coerced and beaten and drugged and kidnapped and detained against their will and stolen from and forced into being presented as prostitutes. Not once (although that would be one too many times). Not twice. But over and over and over again. As Frank Figliuzzi argues in *The Long Haul*, it is misleading to regard trafficked women as freely choosing to be sex workers: "To me, it sounds more like involuntary servitude than free enterprise" (Figliuzzi, 2023). These women and girls are actually not "prostitutes" at all. They are victims of sex trafficking. They are sexual slaves. That's right: 4.5 to 4.75 million women and girls are trafficked for the purpose of sexual slavery each year. And these crimes are hidden behind the thinly veiled and pernicious misnomer "prostitutes."

To put this in perspective, this number is the equivalent to the entire population of the states of Louisiana or Kentucky, or the population of the countries of New Zealand, Ireland, or Costa Rica being sex trafficked every year (U.S. Census Bureau, 2024; World Bank, 2024). And let's remember that in this particular thought experiment, all of the residents of those states and countries would be women and girls. Every year. We need to talk about this. We need to feel a burning hot rage about this widespread gendered violence against women and girls.

Think about this: It is estimated that the entire COVID-19 pandemic caused 7 million deaths over a period of 4 years (World Health Organization, 2024). And we did not tolerate that. We saw it as a global public health crisis. We recognized that it needed to be stopped. And then we took collective action to mobilize every possible resource we had to stop it. What will need to happen for us to take seriously and demand an end to the widespread and endemic sexual violence against women and girls? What will it take for us to recognize this as the global public health and humanitarian crisis that it is? What if the entire population of Ireland was sex trafficked this year? And then all of New Zealand next year? And then Costa Rica? Would we continue to stand by as if helpless to do anything about it? And what if it then spread further, to Kentucky and Louisiana? Would we ask those who were outraged by this to cool down? How is it that we continue to allow this to happen? How has this become normative for us?

The entrenched and longstanding socioeconomic inequalities that women and girls face – many of which are structural and systematically reinforced by governments and religious organizations – further reduce our already limited choice framework (Kristof & WuDunn, 2010; Amnesty International, 2020; United Nations, 2020; World Economic Forum, 2020). This makes it especially important not to allow writing that seeks to reinforce false ideas about prostitution being normal and morally equivalent to paying for parking to go unchecked. Or – even worse - to allow it to be celebrated. And so I have decided that I am not going to cool my poem down. I am going to let the hot rage I feel over this issue fuel me. I am going to keep writing. I am not going to censor myself so that I don't write in a way that is too hot. Because this information should make people uncomfortable. It should force us to ask ourselves, how is it that we are continuing to tolerate this? Why are a literary journal and a university celebrating and showcasing a piece of writing that equates paying for time with a prostitute to paying for parking? We need to change this. We need to do it now. And we need to do it together, with the many people and organizations that are already working tirelessly to combat these crimes against women and girls, and all of those who are trafficked against what should be their basic human rights.

Traffic*

In response to "Parking Meter"

It makes me almost too angry to write
that I spent some of my precious time
- 13 minutes of my life that I'll never get back -
looking up the author's name
because I needed to confirm that the writer is a man
and I wanted to see his face
perhaps even his eyes.

Because in the list
of things to spend money on
"prostitutes"
would never have made it onto any list
I would ever make
about ways to buy time.

If "prostitutes" makes it onto your list
of things
to buy
with money,
what does that make you?

He wrote that he started thinking about the ways we buy time
on this earth
and in among the list of things that seem
in some ways
essential
to life—

things like music
connections to others
time in places we'd want to be
with people we'd want to see
there is this horrible word:
prostitutes.

As if it were as ordinary
as a theme park
or a phone call.

Rent money
the light bill
food.

I hate this poem.
I hate that this word was slipped into a list of things that are otherwise
normal and relatable
it is not.

And so, I ask-
what does that make you?

To have this word on your list
of things to spend money on
to extend your time.

What does that make you?

IN PLAIN SIGHT:
HOW THE EPISTEMOLOGY OF IGNORANCE NORMALIZES GENDER-BASED VIOLENCE

A man who sees women
as commodities
things to be bought
and sold.

The sound of
coins dropping
into
so many
rented holes.

*The poem "Traffic" is a creative work of fiction. The use of the pronoun 'you' within this poem is intended as a universal address to the reader and does not refer to any specific individual. The poem employs poetic license, allowing for creative deviations from conventional language and factual accuracy to enhance its artistic expression. Additionally, the use of metaphor is integral to the poem's imagery and should be interpreted figuratively rather than literally. This work serves as cultural and literary criticism, offering commentary on societal issues through artistic expression.

I Wonder What it is I Am Supposed to Do

How to be safe:

Do not go out alone.

Do not speak to strangers.

(Cover up!)

Do not have desires.

Keep your arms at your sides.

Do not dance.

Do not walk outside.

(Stay home!)

Do not go to parties.

Do not walk by construction sites.

(What are you doing outside!)

Do not sleep at night.

Do not sleep alone.

Do not sleep with the windows open.

Never run alone.

Do not go out in the early morning.

Do not go out at night.

How to be valued:

Be beautiful (but make it look natural).

Be desirable (but leave a little something to the imagination—).

Be inviting (but not a tease).

Be blonde (lucky you!).

Be sexy (but not slutty—*if you know what I mean*).

Be open (but don't talk too much).

Be kind (*c'mon—smile, honey*).

Be fun (not silly, but fun—*you know*).

Be social (but not opinionated).

Be smart (but not too smart).

Be available (since you're not doing anything else anyway).

(If you don't mind, can you just take care of everything).

In the Company of Women

She said
they had sex
that morning—
her face blank
as if she was still bored.

I said
I was worried
about my ovaries—
whether the fullness
was just another cyst
taking hold
inside.

We said
we are so fucking sick of it.

Everyone understood
that "it" really meant all of it—
everything.

Some days
I feel helpless
as I watch
the young girls—

I want to tell them

there is another way

a better way

a different way.

Hunting Grounds

So many days

hours

minutes

seconds

spent

watching

waiting

outside the apartment

the office

at the gas station

lurking in

the grocery store

blending into

the crowd

waiting at the finish line

of the marathon.

A wry

knowing smile

as if

I was

complicit

to blame—

cardless flowers

abandoned

at my doorstep

(I've been here

You can't stop me)

watching

waiting

for me.

And when

I dared

say something—

they said:

but,

he's married

with kids.

These Things

I want to take a moment
to think about these things:

An open window in the summer
a late night trip to the market for ice cream

parking in the campus garage
walking home from work

going for a run in the forest
camping in the woods

having a drink with friends at the bar
helping a stranger

sleeping
smiling
being beautiful
being alone

being poor
needing help
trusting others.

Do not disregard this list
of the most dangerous things
we can do
as women.

IN PLAIN SIGHT:
HOW THE EPISTEMOLOGY OF IGNORANCE NORMALIZES GENDER-BASED VIOLENCE

MARY SIMMERLING

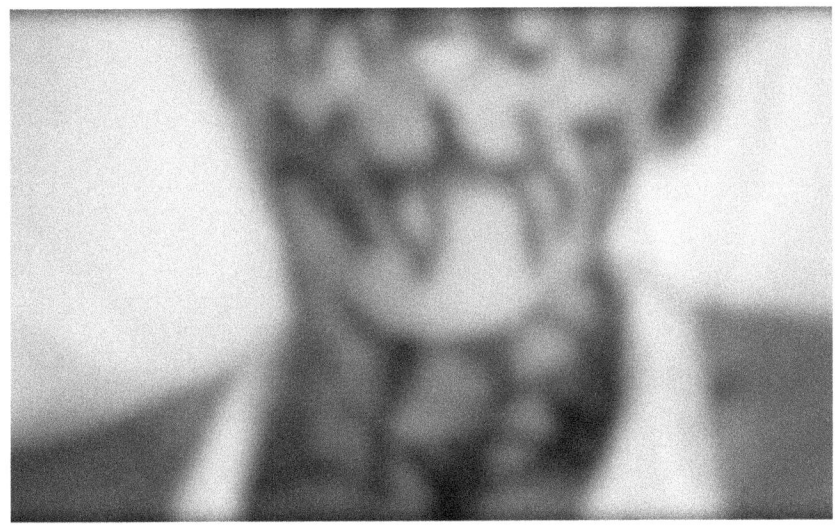

IN PLAIN SIGHT:
HOW THE EPISTEMOLOGY OF IGNORANCE NORMALIZES GENDER-BASED VIOLENCE

Give Us Back Our Names: How Publication Bans Protect Abusers and Silence Victims

A Culture of Complicity

There is nothing about it that is easy. Nothing about it that is acceptable. But there are things that are clear. That is, they are clearer now. And of course, there are things that are wrong. Obviously, unequivocally wrong. There are so many of those things. So many egregious violations. So many ways this particular sexual assault victim — this child — was abandoned, silenced, and blamed by the adults around her. But first, you need to know that - despite the headlines - this is not the main story: "Alice Munro stayed with her husband after she had been told he sexually abused her daughter" (Mannie, 2024). While true, it is misleading about the scope of the actual harms that took place. This headline minimizes the broader, systemic harms that occurred in the aftermath of Gerald Fremlin's sexual abuse of his stepdaughter, Andrea Skinner, when she was just 9 years old, including the subsequent choices of those who knew about the abuse and chose to ignore or bury it.

There is also the matter of who is responsible for the harms Andrea suffered and who—in their willful silence and abandonment of Andrea—is also complicit in them. Because it wasn't just Gerald Fremlin. Of course, Gerald Fremlin is the one who sexually abused Andrea. But then there is the cascade of harms that came in the aftermath. It was also Andrea's father James Munro, who Andrea told about the abuse immediately after it happened. And what did James Munro do to protect his young daughter? He sent her back to Gerald Fremlin, this time accompanied by his two other daughters. This response is both unimaginable and unconscionable to me.

So yes, Alice did stay with her husband Gerald Fremlin after her own daughter—a nine-year-old victim of sexual abuse by Munro's then 52-year-old husband Fremlin—told her of the abuse many years after it had taken place (Skinner, 2024). But this was not a secret. Many, many people knew about it. As Andrea herself wrote in her 2024 essay in *The Toronto Star*, "Children are still silenced far too often. In my case, my mother's fame meant that the secrecy spread far beyond the family. Many influential people came to know something of my story yet continued to support, and add to, a narrative they knew was false." This silencing has a chilling effect on survivors. As I wrote in the introduction to *We've Been Put Through Fire & Come Out Divine*, "Our voices have been silenced for so long. We have been told that our truths aren't true, and that even if they are, no one cares anyway. And in response, we have hidden, made ourselves small, and become silent and invisible."

Mechanisms & Psychological Impacts of Silencing Survivors

This silencing is not just a personal betrayal; it's a societal one. It's a narrative that tells survivors everywhere that their stories are secondary to the reputations of those who harm them. Rachel Louise Snyder, in *No Visible Bruises*, discusses how abuse often persists in silence until the severity is undeniable. In Andrea's case, each occasion of silence and complicity contributed to a narrative that prioritized the reputation of the abuser and those associated with him over the welfare of the victim.

Silencing has devastating effects on survivors. It's not just about Andrea being told to keep quiet; it's about every survivor who has been told to stay silent for their own good, for the good of the family, or to protect their abuser's reputation. Silencing is itself a form of violence. Research shows that being silenced can cause immense psychological harms, reinforcing trauma and worsening symptoms of PTSD and depression (Ullman, 2023). In her book *Trauma and Recovery*, Judith Herman (2015) demonstrates that being silenced and having one's truth denied or buried is a continuation of the abuse. This silencing sends a strong signal to the victim that their pain isn't valid, that their experience doesn't matter, and that their voice isn't worthy of being heard. Thus, silence and secrecy are employed as powerful weapons of abuse.

When legal measures like publication bans are used to enforce silence, they are often justified as being in the best interests of the victim. However, they frequently serve to protect the abuser more than the victim. Publication bans can reinforce a culture of silence, shielding perpetrators from public accountability and preventing survivors from reclaiming their voices and stories. Survivors who are silenced by these bans often suffer increased feelings of isolation, shame, and helplessness. Thus the legal system can end up perpetuating trauma rather than protecting against it. And this is not just about what happened to Andrea; it's about a system that routinely silences victims under the guise of providing protection.

Public Perception and the Erasure of Victims' Voices

Both Alice Munro and Gerald Fremlin are now deceased, and Andrea Skinner is in her 50s. Gerald Fremlin was found guilty in 2005 of sexually abusing Andrea in 1976 (Butt, 2024). When Gerald Fremlin was found guilty 19 years ago, both Alice and her husband, Gerald Fremlin, were still alive. It wasn't until years later—in 2013—that Alice won the Nobel Prize. During all that time—all of those years and decades—Alice's name and her stories were publicly celebrated, while Andrea's name and story were silenced under a publication ban to "protect" her. But who was really being protected? The victim, or the narrative that shielded a famous writer and her circle?

In the aftermath of Munro's recent death, I heard a radio program on CBC interviewing her biographer Robert Thacker (Nichols, 2024). He spoke so lovingly about her, as if she had been this perfect Canadian mother and author. This was just after her death. His biography of Alice Munro came out in 2011. Now he's admitting that he knew, too. All those years ago. He knew. Thacker has defended his decision to withhold this information from his 2011 biography of Munro because he says it wasn't that kind of book. What kind of book is that? Apparently it was a biography of her that it wasn't supposed to be salacious. And so now I want to know how is it that the sexual abuse of a child could be considered salacious? But Thacker is not the only one. Many, many others also knew. Giants in the literary and publishing communities knew. Andrea brought her story to the press. They buried it. Deep. They silenced her. Over and over and over again Andrea was left to believe that her story didn't matter. That it wasn't to be believed. And that even if it was true—which of course was proven in 2005 when Gerald Fremlin's own writings to then young Andrea were used to substantiate the charges against him—that no one actually cared anyway.

And what did Gerald Fremlin have to say? He said that he was the victim. And Alice Munro? She told her daughter that she viewed it as infidelity and blamed Andrea for enticing and seducing 52-year-old Fremlin. As a reminder, Andrea was 9 at the time. And what did Fremlin do? In a flimsy and perverse attempt to defend himself, Fremlin invoked Nabokov. Fremlin said that he was Humbert Humbert and that Andrea was Lolita. He claimed that *he* was in fact the victim. But it's not like that. It didn't happen like that. Not at all. Plus, he's missed the whole point of *Lolita*. And by once again attempting to weaponize literature against his victim and cloak himself in a twisted and mistaken reading of Nabokov, he revealed himself for what he truly is.

In 2005, Gerald Fremlin pled guilty and was given a suspended sentence and probation for two years on the charge of indecent assault, a criminal offence from the 1970s that preceded the current charge of sexual assault under the Canadian legal system. He was given probation. For sexually assaulting a 9 year old girl. And the names of the parties involved were put under a publication ban. To protect them. At this point Andrea was 38, and Fremlin was 80. And I have to wonder - who was it that needed protection at that point?

Publication Bans: Tools of Protection or Oppression?

While publication bans and nondisclosure agreements (NDAs) are touted as protective measures for victims, they can do more to protect perpetrators than victims. This is because they can present powerful barriers to victims' abilities to seek justice and reclaim our stories. They not only have the effect of silencing victims, but also shielding abusers from accountability. A recent case in which an adult survivor shared her story with her supporters resulted in her being fined by the courts when the perpetrator found out that she had shared her story (Mandel, 2021). In cases like this we must ask the hard questions, who are these bans protecting? And who are they harming?

If the intention of these bans is to protect survivors, why are survivors often left feeling even more isolated and abandoned? Why are these tools being used to prevent survivors from reclaiming their own stories? These bans can do more harm than good, creating barriers that prevent survivors from speaking out and seeking justice. Publication bans don't just silence the victims – taking away their ability to choose for themselves yet again — these bans allow perpetrators to potentially continue their abusive behaviors in the shadows and shielded from the scrutiny that could prevent further harm. The implications of publication bans are staggering. By silencing victims we aren't just failing them, we're systematically enabling a cycle of abuse to continue. Meanwhile, the public remains largely unaware of the real dangers posed by perpetrators who often remain in positions of power and enjoy a false reputation in the eyes of the public, as Gerald Fremlin most certainly did.

Legal Reforms - Restoring Survivor Agency

It's time we look into legal reforms that actually protect survivors rather than take our agency away from us again. A good place to start would be by giving us back our names and our stories, or at least giving us a straightforward method to do that once we reach the age of majority and can make those choices as an adult. While some of these publication bans no doubt came from well-meaning places, the durability of them over time has the potential to cause additional harms later. More nuanced and appropriate uses of publication bans to protect minors and others who actually need and want that protection is worth exploring. Another area in need of attention is the use of anti-defamation lawsuits to silence survivors who speak out or attempt to seek justice. As Mandi Gray argues in her groundbreaking book *Suing for Silence*, defamation law is being weaponized to silence survivors and advocates who speak out about sexual violence, perpetuating the myth that false allegations of sexual violence are common and enabling abusive men to use defamation lawsuits against those who seek to hold them accountable.

We deserve better. Andrea Skinner deserved better. She deserved to be heard, believed, and supported. Instead, she was silenced and ignored. And it was done under the auspices of protecting her.

It's time we take back our voices. It's time to reclaim our stories. And to do it with our own words. In our own names.

Requiem for Girls

Because there is
the frailty—

secrets whispered
through silent breaths

the blood
that pulses
and spills

that is not
entirely mine

the longing
of the heart
the way it yearns—
let me beat
just one
last time

I watch as
losses
pile up
like stones
threatening
to weigh me down.

And my own fear

that they will

somehow

trace a silent path

deep

inside of me

a pile of ash—

the remnants of

so many fires.

Remains

A spatter of blood
in the white snow

centered among
slight depressions

where feathers
at the very tips
of wings

touched down
ever so briefly

talons grabbing
prey

a rabbit's tracks
and mine.

I remember
an article I read
last week

about men
who stalk women
who run trails—

WINNIFRED TEO
[MARCH 29, 1967 - MAY 22, 1985]

KARINA VETRANO
[JULY 12, 1986 - AUGUST 2, 2016]

ELIZA FLETCHER
[NOVEMBER 9, 1987 - SEPTEMBER 2, 2022]

VANESSA MARCOTTE
[JUNE 17, 1989 - AUGUST 7, 2016]

MOLLIE TIBBITS
[MAY 8, 1998 - JULY 18, 2018]

LAKEN RILEY
[JANUARY 2002 - FEBRUARY 22, 2024]

My stolen sisters

I carry you
folded in prayer
never again—

Rats

First
we vilify them
hunt them down
feed them poison
celebrate their demise.

Then we breed them
in labs
knocking out
what's theirs
replacing it with
what's ours--
our cancers
our degenerations
our illnesses.

Dissecting them
searching for clues
to make us whole

to reveal secrets
of all the things
that plague us.

Yesterday
I found a study

it showed that rats
experiencing "predatory events"
show changes
for generations.

It read: "Our data illustrate that a surprisingly small amount of preconception predator stress alters the brain, physiology, and behavior of future generations. A better understanding of the 'long shadow' cast by fearful events is critical for understanding the adaptive costs and benefits of transgenerational plasticity. It also suggests the intriguing possibility that similar risk-induced changes are the rule rather than the exception in free-living organisms, and that such multigenerational impacts are as ubiquitous as they are cryptic" (Bhattacharya et al., 2023).

Ubiquitous
cryptic
generational
costs and benefits

traumas
long shadows.

IN PLAIN SIGHT:
HOW THE EPISTEMOLOGY OF IGNORANCE NORMALIZES GENDER-BASED VIOLENCE

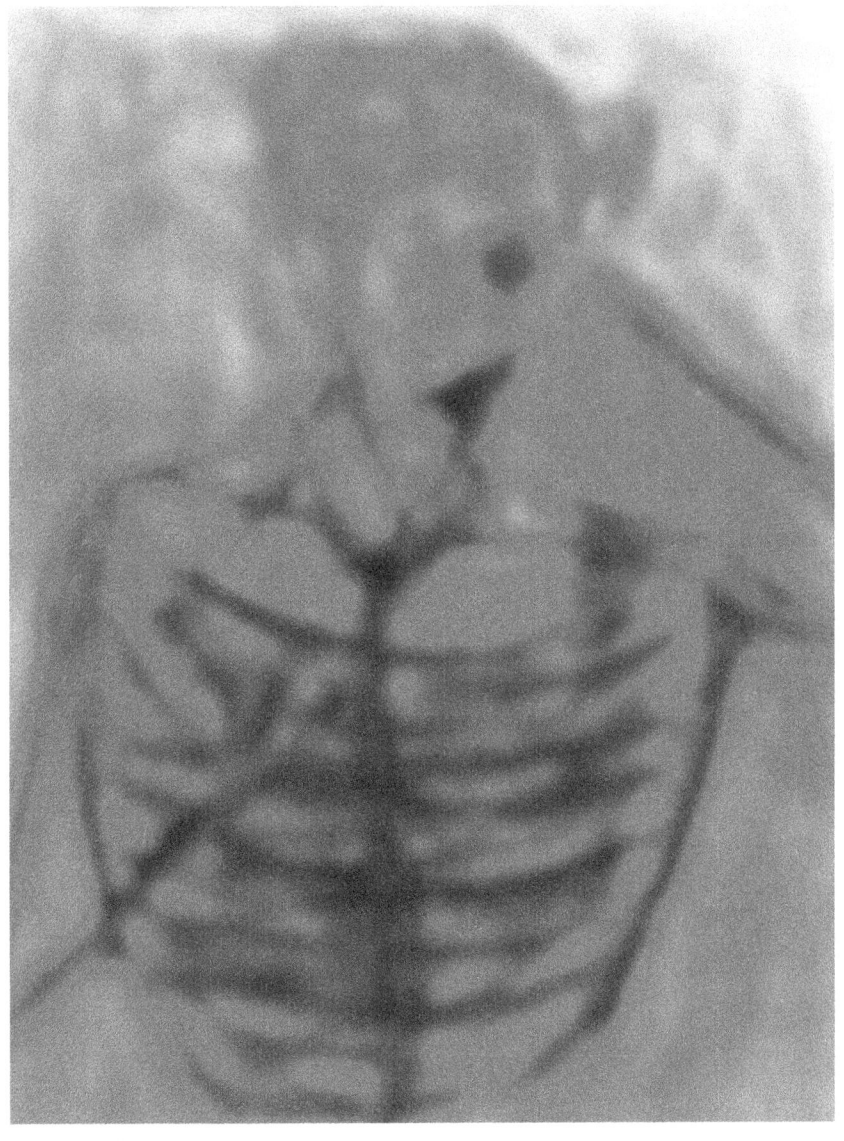

IN PLAIN SIGHT:
HOW THE EPISTEMOLOGY OF IGNORANCE NORMALIZES GENDER-BASED VIOLENCE

Nothing to See Here: Online Pornography and the Normalization of Sexual Violence

Pornography's Role in Shaping Social Norms

In the 21st century, online pornography has become a pervasive force in shaping societal norms, with widespread implications for individual behavior and broader cultural attitudes. The accessibility of pornography—now available to anyone with a device, at any hour of the day or night—has led to its deep entrenchment in everyday life. Recent research shows that porn sites are getting more visitors than Amazon, X (formerly Twitter), and Netflix combined, demonstrating the alarming scale of its use (Mehmood Qadri et al., 2023). In 2019, the world's top porn site's traffic jumped to one billion visitors per month, placing it among the world's top internet sites (Donadelli and Lalane, 2020). The rise of increasingly violent forms of online pornography has become a significant social concern, particularly in its potential to impact the behavior of its consumers and, consequently, exacerbate the widespread problem of sexual violence, especially against women. Pornography plays a significant role in normalizing violence against women and girls, and it is especially dangerous because of the many ways in which it is presented as "victimless" with "willing" participants. Make no mistake: pornography is not victimless. It often involves trafficking, coercion, exploitation, rape, and significant psychological, emotions, and physical harms, primarily to women and girls (Mehmood Qadri et al., 2023). It damages not only the individual women and girls who are directly subjected to it, but all women and girls who are then seen through its toxic lens.

Peggy Orenstein (2021), in an article for *The New York Times*, highlights the concerning trend of violence in online pornography, citing a 2020 analysis of over 4,000 heterosexual scenes on two of the largest pornography websites, Pornhub and Xvideos. The analysis found that 45% of the scenes on Pornhub and 35% on Xvideos contained aggression, with this aggression almost exclusively directed at women. This stark revelation underscores the normalization of violent behavior in the context of sexuality, suggesting that pornography is no longer just a depiction of sexual acts, but an active model for behavior in intimate relationships. The modeling of violent sexual behaviors within pornography poses profound ethical and social concerns. The porn industry perpetuates a narrative where sexual violence against women is not only depicted, but portrayed as normative sexual expression. Recent research has established a correlation between repeated exposure to violent pornography and an increased acceptance of sexual aggression (Wright et al., 2016). For instance, a study published in the *Archives of Sexual Behavior* found that male adolescents exposed to violent pornography were over three times more likely to perpetrate sexual aggression compared to their non-exposed peers (Rostad et al., 2019). The association remained significant even after controlling for variables such as substance use and attitudes toward gender roles. The implications of these findings are dire, suggesting that pornography in fact reshapes the understanding of consent, intimacy, and sexual relations, often trivializing or excusing the violence inflicted upon women.

This normalization extends beyond explicit materials into mainstream media and popular culture. The film *Boys Don't Cry* (1999), for example, vividly and painfully illustrates the horrific real-world consequences of societal complicity, toxic masculinity, and violent transphobia, which are mirrored and magnified in contemporary online pornography. In a conversation with philosopher and author Amia Srinivasan, Michelle Goldberg (2021) posed critical questions regarding pornography's impact on the societal understanding of women. Goldberg inquired whether pornography, rather than simply depicting the subordination of women, might actually play a role in making this subordination a reality. Srinivasan's response was unequivocal: "Yes, yes to all of it." According to Srinivasan, pornography not only reflects but actively reinforces the objectification and marginalization of women, making it complicit in a culture that normalizes and legitimizes their exploitation. This insight challenges the idea that pornography merely mirrors societal norms—it is a powerful agent in shaping them.

Adlerian Psychology and the Masculine Protest

Alfred Adler, the founder of Adlerian psychology, recognized the profound psychological and societal effects of inequality between men and women. He proposed that many of the mental health issues experienced by women, particularly those labeled as "hysteria" in the early 20th century, were not the result of inherent pathology, but rather the consequences of the oppressive social structures that confined women to subordinate roles. Adler argued that the hysteria often seen in women was symptomatic of the broader psychological distress caused by living in a patriarchal society that restricted women's agency and autonomy. In Adler's view, women's suffering was a direct result of the societal inequities they faced, not a flaw in their psychological constitution.

Central to Adlerian theory is the concept of the "masculine protest" (Griffith & Maybell, 2020). This idea posits that individuals, particularly men, assert dominance over others as a way of compensating for feelings of inferiority. For men in a patriarchal society, this protest manifests as a constant effort to prove their superiority by asserting control over women and relegating them to subordinate roles. In the context of pornography, this masculine protest is evident in the ways in which women are reduced to mere objects for male sexual gratification. This reduction is not a mere representation in media, but a harmful reinforcement of power dynamics that dehumanize and objectify women. Adlerian psychologist Susan Belangee (2020) has further explored the consequences of the "excessive pre-eminence of manliness" in patriarchal societies, noting that the overemphasis on masculinity fosters an environment that glorifies male dominance and aggression, while devaluing feminine traits of equality, empathy, and cooperation. This societal imbalance not only harms women but also perpetuates toxic masculine behaviors, including the normalization of violence. In this framework, pornography, with its pervasive depictions of sexual aggression and objectification, becomes a tool that reinforces the gendered inequalities that lie at the heart of patriarchy.

The Toxic Impact of Pornography and the Need for Change

To address the harmful impact of pornography on the equality between men and women, an Adlerian approach suggests that we must begin by addressing the root causes of the masculine protest and the pervasive dominance of masculinity in patriarchal society. This means confronting the ways in which societal structures and cultural norms continually uphold and reinforce male superiority. Pornography is both a symptom of these broader issues and a contributing factor in their perpetuation. One crucial step in addressing the harm caused by pornography is through a widespread educational initiative aimed at dismantling the toxic ideologies embedded in patriarchal culture. Such an initiative would focus on promoting gender equality, diversity, and inclusion, while simultaneously raising awareness of the harmful effects of pornography, especially in its objectification of women. This educational effort would involve teaching individuals, particularly young people, about the ethical and emotional dimensions of intimacy, consent, and respect, emphasizing that sexual violence is never justified and is never acceptable. In the Adlerian tradition, healing and change begin with the recognition of shared human dignity and the importance of social connection. To move beyond the harmful cycle of objectification and violence perpetuated by pornography, society must foster environments where women are not seen as objects but as autonomous individuals with inherent worth. This requires not only deconstructing the narratives perpetuated by the pornography industry but also shifting cultural attitudes toward a more inclusive and respectful model of sexuality.

The ubiquity of online pornography and its increasing normalization of violence against women is a pressing social issue that demands attention. As demonstrated by the work of Adler and contemporary feminist theorists such as Susanne Kappele, this problem cannot be viewed as an isolated issue but must be understood in the context of broader societal inequalities. To address the harm caused by pornography, we must challenge the entrenched patriarchal structures that perpetuate gendered violence and promote harmful cultural norms. This will require a comprehensive societal shift—one that moves away from toxic masculinity and toward a more egalitarian and respectful understanding of sexuality. Education, empathy, and collective responsibility are key to dismantling the harmful effects of pornography and creating a society where women are not reduced to mere objects for male gratification, but are valued for their autonomy, dignity, and humanity.

Monster

for Aileen Wuornos

In the theatre
they did not miss
one handful of popcorn

as they watched him
(projected in widescreen
with full dolby surround)

repeatedly rape her
first with his own body
and then again
with a steel pipe.

The Haunting Hours

I leaned over and fumbled for the clock
wondering whether it was morning yet
checking the big window for any light peeking through

knowing that sometimes
and especially these days
the way the snow throws up the moon's shine
can easily mimic the dawn.

I decided instead
to just breathe
knowing as I did
that this would calm me down
and place me where I was
safely in my own bed
awake and alert
once again
in the haunting hours.

That night I had been asleep
my son stretched out alongside me
smelling of the creek and the forest
and the promises of spring.

I hadn't been afraid that night
I hadn't even known about him

I hadn't seen his face yet
or the confidence in the set of his jaw
as he walked about in the dark.

It had been overcast and rainy for days
and when the sun finally rose in its early morning brilliance
it lit up the row of windows overlooking the pond
I screamed in terror at the line of smeared handprints
now visible at the very center of each otherwise
perfectly clean window.

And then, of course, there were the scant, smudged
glove marks in the bedroom
and the muddied footprint at the edge of the window well
where he lost his footing and slipped
as he reached over to test the sash.

The police were no help
not at first anyway
and then afterwards—
when I called again later,
I knew I could never call them again.

I hadn't been afraid that night
the fear came for me later
after he had already left
when I knew he'd been there

when I understood that he'd been hunting me
all those months—

watching

waiting

learning

getting to know my dog.

There were the beer cans near the shed
that I had assumed were the painters'
the night sensor that had stopped working
the small hole in the fence
the feeling I had every time I walked past the tall yellow waders
the ones that had remained hanging untouched all those months
on a single hook in the wall
just next to the door in the basement.

When we finally packed up to move,
I found the hole that he had cut
hidden as it had been all of that time
just behind the waders.

In Plain Sight

The nurse said—

last week there were seven of them

seven women

who had been brought in

by their parents

their friends

taken from their children.

Women who's necks

had been held

with hands

and with belts

fastened—

their buckles leaving

square bruises

centered in

petechiae

like blood spatter

swollen

purple

and yellow

and green

IN PLAIN SIGHT:
HOW THE EPISTEMOLOGY OF IGNORANCE NORMALIZES GENDER-BASED VIOLENCE

crescent moon shapes

scaling

the full length

of the neck—

she said it takes

just 10 seconds

but then again

that is for men—

for women it is

faster

more intense

there is more strength

working against them

more force

larger hands

on men

who hunt

women

in their homes.

And I wonder

what it is

that makes a man

want a woman

to suffer

so much—

to see fear

in her eyes

to watch her

desperately

grasping

for life.

All the mothers

left kneeling

in the ruins

at altars of despair

knowing that—

each man

once had

a mother

of his own.

In loving memory of my mother in law, Cynthia Ann Hanegan (1947 - 1974), who I never had the chance to meet.

Sparrows on a Clothesline

after Anne Carson's "Desert Town"

This is not what was supposed to happen
it was not supposed to be like this
not at all—

and yet here we are
already
unrecognizable.

I know I will not
be able to stop it.

All I can do
is to keep writing
to keep making space
to remain focused
on what I can do
to keep naming
the violence.

I wake before sunrise
the birds are starting to return again
I listen for them in the dark
I wonder what will happen
to them—

and of course the trees

and the squirrels

the salmon

and the waterways

the forests

and the mountains

the deserts

and the towns

the women

and the children.

Because I know

that no one

nothing—

will be spared

in this cutting away.

Thought Experiment

Try this:
imagine a world
where rape
was as despised
as deplorable
contemptible
unacceptable
as morally reprehensible
as lynching.

Imagine a day
where violence
against women
was repugnant
rather than ordinary

was tragic
catastrophic
and heartbreaking
rather than entertaining

where women were no longer
bought and sold
like so much chattel

were no longer just
so many
rented holes.

And now:
try it at home

try it in the morning
over coffee
with toast

try it at the office
next to the flag
in the boardroom
the classroom

try it in the emergency room
and the courtroom

try it in the nightclub
the bathroom
the coatroom.

Try it at the bar
and the table
try it over
dessert.
Try it
in the evening
before bed
with your partner
your spouse
your children

and grandchildren.
Try it in the barracks
and on the battlefield.

Try it on the bus
the train
the plane.

Try it in the alley
and in your car.

Try it in the gym
on the playground
the football field
the basketball court.

Try it at school
and at church.

Try it everywhere
the implicit endorsement
of violence against women
is allowed to linger and lurk.

IN PLAIN SIGHT:
HOW THE EPISTEMOLOGY OF IGNORANCE NORMALIZES GENDER-BASED VIOLENCE

MARY SIMMERLING

Resources

1. Polaris Project: A leading organization in the global fight to eradicate modern slavery and restore freedom to survivors.

2. RAINN (Rape, Abuse & Incest National Network): The largest anti-sexual violence organization in the U.S. operating the National Sexual Assault Hotline.

3. Take Back the Night Foundation: An international organization with the mission of ending sexual violence in all forms, including sexual assault, sexual abuse, trafficking, stalking, and harassment.

4. End Violence Against Women International: A non-profit organization dedicated to improving criminal justice and community responses to sexual assault.

5. SASS Go (Survivors' Anti-Trafficking Safe Space Global Outreach): SASS Go is an organization dedicated to eradicating sexual assault and sex trafficking while empowering survivors through various programs, resources, and advocacy.

6. UN Women: The United Nations entity dedicated to gender equality and the empowerment of women, working to address violence against women and girls.

7. International Justice Mission (IJM): A global organization that protects the poor from violence throughout the developing world.

8. National Human Trafficking Hotline: A 24/7, confidential hotline for

victims and survivors of human trafficking in the U.S.

9. Coalition Against Trafficking in Women (CATW): An international non-governmental organization that opposes human trafficking and sexual exploitation in all forms.

10. Love146: An international human rights organization working to end child trafficking and exploitation through survivor care and prevention.

11. Shared Hope International: Works to prevent sex trafficking, restore and empower survivors, and bring justice to vulnerable adults and children.

12. Truckers Against Trafficking: An organization that trains truck drivers and other transportation professionals to recognize and report instances of human trafficking.

13. The Global Women's Institute (GWI): Engages in research and education to improve the lives of women and girls globally.

14. Women's Aid: A federation of over 180 organizations providing support to women and children experiencing domestic violence in the UK.

15. International Rescue Committee (IRC): Responds to the world's worst humanitarian crises, helping to restore health, safety, education, economic well being, and power to people devastated by conflict and disaster, including women and girls.

16. Equality Now: An international human rights organization using the law to protect and promote the rights of women and girls around the world.

17. UNICEF: Works to promote and protect the rights of children worldwide, including efforts to combat violence against girls.

18. The NO MORE Foundation: Dedicated to ending domestic violence and sexual assault by increasing awareness and inspiring action.

IN PLAIN SIGHT:
HOW THE EPISTEMOLOGY OF IGNORANCE NORMALIZES GENDER-BASED VIOLENCE

References and Further Reading

Amnesty International. (2020). *Tackling the global crisis: Gender inequality and women's rights*. Retrieved from https://www.amnesty.org/en/latest/research/2020/03/tackling-the-global-crisis-gender-inequality-and-womens-rights/

Atwood, M. (1985). *The Handmaid's Tale*. McClelland & Stewart.

Belangee, S. (2020). Celebrating 150 years: A president's perspective. *The Journal of Individual Psychology,* 76(1), 4-5.

Bhattacharya, S., MacCallum, P. E., Dayma, M., McGrath-Janes, A., King, B., Dawson, L., Bambico, F. R., Berry, M. D., Yuan, Q., Martin, G. M., Preisser, E. L., & Blundell, J. J. (2023). A short pre-conception bout of predation risk affects both children and grandchildren. *Scientific Reports,* 13(1), 10886. https://doi.org/10.1038/s41598-023-37455-9

Bluvshtein, M. (2020). Individual psychology as a "living force of progress." *The Journal of Individual Psychology,* 76(1), 6-20. https://doi.org/10.1353/jip.2020.0011

Butt, M. (2024). Nobel-winning writer's daughter reveals she was sexually abused by stepfather and her mom stayed with him. *The Independent.* Available at: https://www.independent.co.uk

Carson, A. (1995). Desert Town. In *Plainwater: Essays and Poetry* (pp. 123-124). Knopf.

Donadelli, M., & Lalanne, M. (2020). Sex and "the City": Financial stress and online pornography consumption. *Journal of Behavioral and Experimental Finance*, 27, 100379. https://doi.org/10.1016/j.jbef.2020.100379

Figliuzzi, F. (2023). *The long haul: How to keep going when the going gets tough*. Harper.

Goldberg, M. (2021, September 24). Why sex-positive feminism is falling out of fashion. *The New York Times*.

Gray, M. (2023). *Suing for silence*. Fernwood Publishing.

Griffith, J., & Maybell, S. A. (2020). Adler's original contributions to psychology. *The Journal of Individual Psychology*, 76(1), 21-30.

Herman, J. (2015). *Trauma and recovery: The aftermath of violence—from domestic abuse to political terror*. Basic Books.

International Labour Organization. (2017). *Global estimates of modern slavery: Forced labour and forced marriage*. Retrieved from [https://www.ilo.org/global/topics/forced-labour/publications/WCMS_575479/lang--en/index.htm]

Jenkins, P. (Director). (2003). *Monster* [Film]. Media 8 Entertainment; Denver and Delilah Films; K/W Productions.

Kappeler, S. (1986). *The pornography of representation*. Polity Press.

Kristof, N. D., & WuDunn, S. (2010). *Half the sky: Turning oppression into opportunity for women worldwide*. Vintage Books.

Mandel, M. (2021, March 19). Sex assault victim fined $2,000 for violating pub ban on her own name. *The Toronto Sun*.

Mannie, K. (2024). Alice Munro stayed with husband who sexually abused her daughter: Essay. *Global News*.

Mehmood Qadri, H., Waheed, A., Munawar, A., Saeed, H., Abdullah, S., Munawar, T., Luqman, S., Saffi, J., Ahmad, A., & Babar, M. S. (2023). Physiological, Psychosocial and Substance Abuse Effects of Pornography Addiction: A Narrative Review. *Cureus,* 15(1), e33703. https://doi.org/10.7759/cureus.33703

Mills, C. W. (1997). *The racial contract*. Cornell University Press.

Nabokov, V. (1955). *Lolita*. Olympia Press.

Nichols, A. (Host). (2024, May 14). *CBC News Network's Andrew Nichols speaks with Alice Munro biographer Robert Thacker* [Video]. CBC Radio. https://www.cbc.ca/player/play/video/9.4226515

Orenstein, P. (2021, June 14). If you ignore porn, you aren't teaching sex ed. *The New York Times*.

Pateman, C. (1988). *The sexual contract*. Stanford University Press.

Peirce, K. (Director). (1999). *Boys don't cry* [Film]. Fox Searchlight Pictures.

Polaris Project. (2020). *The facts*. Retrieved from https://polarisproject.org/human-trafficking/facts/

Rostad, W. L., Gittins-Stone, D., Huntington, C., Rizzo, C. J., Pearlman, D., & Orchowski, L. (2019). The Association Between Exposure to Violent Pornography and Teen Dating Violence in Grade 10 High School Students. *Archives of sexual behavior*, 48(7), 2137–2147. https://doi.org/10.1007/s10508-019-1435-4

Reuters. (2024, December 11). Human trafficking rises sharply after dropping during pandemic, UN says. Retrieved from https://www.reuters.com/world/human-trafficking-rises-sharply-after-dropping-during-pandemic-un-says-2024-12-11

Silva, D. (2024, November 20). Man found guilty of murdering Georgia nursing student Laken Riley, sentenced to life. *NBC News*. https://www.nbcnews.com/news/us-news/prosecutors-say-dna-fingerprints-show-jose-ibarra-killed-laken-riley-rcna180316

Simmerling, M. (Ed.). (2024). *We've been put through fire & come out divine*. Amherst Writers & Artists Press.

Simmerling, M. (Ed.). (2024). *We've got some things to say: Reshaping narratives around sexual violence*. Amherst Writers & Artists Press.

Skinner, A. R. (2024). "My stepfather sexually abused me when I was a child. My mother, Alice Munro, chose to stay with him." *The Toronto Star*.

Snyder, R. L. (2019). *No visible bruises: What we don't know about domestic violence can kill us*. Bloomsbury Publishing.

Thacker, R. (2011). *Alice Munro: Writing her lives*. Emblem Editions.

Thompson, N. (2024). "Literary world grapples with revelation Alice Munro stayed with her daughter's abuser." *The Canadian Press.*

Tuck, D. M. (2014). Parking meter. *Rattle.* Retrieved from https://www.rattle.com/parking-meter-by-dean-marshall-tuck/

Ullman, S. E. (2003). *Social reactions to child sexual abuse disclosures: A critical review.* Journal of Child Sexual Abuse, 12(1), 89-121. https://doi.org/10.1300/J070v12n01_05

U.S. Census Bureau. (2024). *State populations.* Retrieved from https://www.census.gov

U.S. Department of State. (2021). *Trafficking in persons report.* Retrieved from https://www.state.gov/trafficking-in-persons-report/

United Nations. (2020). *The world's women 2020: Trends and statistics.* Retrieved from https://unstats.un.org/unsd/demographic-social/products/dyb/documents/ww2020.pdf

United Nations. (n.d.). *Understanding human trafficking.* Retrieved from https://www.un.org/en/peace-and-security/understanding-human-trafficking

United Nations Office on Drugs and Crime. (2020). *Global report on trafficking in persons.* Retrieved from https://www.unodc.org/unodc/data-and-analysis/glotip.html

United Nations Office on Drugs and Crime. (2024, December). *Global human trafficking report: Detected victims up 25% as more children are exploited and forced labor cases spike*. Retrieved from https://www.unodc.org/unodc/en/press/releases/2024/December/unodc-global-human-trafficking-report_-detected-victims-up-25-per-cent-as-more-children-are-exploited-and-forced-labour-cases-spike.html

United States Advisory Council on Human Trafficking. (2024). *Annual report 2024*. Retrieved from https://www.state.gov/wp-content/uploads/2024/03/2024-Council-Annual-Report_508-FINAL.pdf

World Bank. (2024). *Country populations*. Retrieved from https://data.worldbank.org/indicator/SP.POP.TOTL

World Economic Forum. (2020). *Global gender gap report*. Retrieved from https://www.weforum.org/reports/gender-gap-2020-report-100-years-pay-equality

World Health Organization. (2024). *WHO Coronavirus (COVID-19) Dashboard*. Retrieved from https://covid19.who.int/

Wright, P. J., Tokunaga, R. S., & Kraus, A. (2016). A meta-analysis of pornography consumption and actual acts of sexual aggression in general population studies. *Journal of Communication*, 66(1), 183–205. https://doi.org/10.1111/jcom.12201

Yourish, K., Daniel, A., Datar, S., White, I., & Gamio, L. (2025, March 7). "These words are disappearing in the new Trump administration." *The New York Times*. https://www.nytimes.com/interactive/2025/03/07/us/trump-federal-agencies-websites-words-dei.html

www.ingramcontent.com/pod-product-compliance
Lightning Source LLC
Chambersburg PA
CBHW051602010526
44118CB00023B/2785